The 10-Minute Pause
for Busy Teachers

Bringing More Fulfillment to Your Work and Life

JULIE SCHMIDT HASSON

First Published 2023
By Chalk and Chances, LLC
P.O. Box 611
Boone, NC 28608

ISBN: 979-8-218-11510-4

9 798218 115104

Getting Started

Teaching has never been more challenging. Trying to meet the needs of diverse learners with limited time and resources can deplete even the most dedicated teacher. One simple strategy for regaining energy is a pause. Turning off the noise for just 10 minutes can restore peace and balance. Creating a routine around the pause in the morning and evening brings the comfort of predictability in an otherwise chaotic time. Ongoing reflection can help you make a greater and more consistent impact on students and find more satisfaction in teaching.

A morning routine sets the tone for the day, empowering you to define the day rather than allowing the day to be defined by events and circumstances. A morning routine brings a sense of calm and predictability, especially during challenging seasons. The mind is like a blank canvas in the morning, and adding a bit of inspiration to that canvas can impact the entire day. Each morning page has the following prompts, which prime your mind to prepare for a peaceful and productive day.

How do I want my students to feel today?
Deciding how you want students to feel leads you to act and interact in ways that elicit those feelings. For example, if you want your students to feel confident, you are more likely to notice and praise their effort. If you want your students to feel safe, you will take action to create a classroom free from humiliation or rejection.

How do I want to feel today?
When you choose how you want to feel (instead of letting circumstances determine your mood), you focus on things that elicit those feelings. For example, if you want to feel peaceful, you are less likely to get agitated by the behavior of others. If you want to feel connected, you are more likely to engage with others.

What is my intention for the day?
When you determine your intention for the day, you define success for yourself. You choose a marker of success within your control, rather than allowing external forces to judge your success. For example, your intention may be to help your students feel more competent rather than achieve higher test scores. Your intention may be to try a new strategy, even if you don't implement it perfectly.

What do you want to accomplish today?
You have big goals and dreams, and those are realized through daily actions. It's easy to get off track when the urgency of others overtakes what is important to you. Instead of letting others own your day, schedule some time for your priorities. When it comes to your list, less is more. Focus on a few specific action steps tied to your big goals.

An evening routine helps you release the day's stress and prepare for rest. A consistent evening routine reduces late-night anxiety, staving off the thoughts that keep you awake. Each evening page contains the following prompts to help you end the day with peace and perspective.

What were my students' wins today?

Students are evolving, and their success is rarely a perfect, positive trajectory. They will have ups and downs, and focusing on their small wins can strengthen your patience as you help them grow toward their potential. Focusing on their wins can also help you see evidence of your impact.

What were my wins today?

Just like your students, you are imperfect and evolving. Give yourself the same grace you show to others. The day may not have gone as you hoped, but even the most difficult day has some wins. Did you submit attendance without a reminder? Did you keep the classroom fish alive? Celebrate those victories.

What am I learning?

The world is constantly changing, and one of the most effective ways to handle change is embracing continuous learning. Seeing yourself as a learner helps you cultivate new skills and adapt. If you're always learning, you're always improving, and you can derive satisfaction and excitement from your new knowledge and skills.

What made me feel grateful today?

Regularly practicing gratitude by taking time to notice and reflect upon the things for which you're thankful creates more joy, resilience, and better physical and mental health. Gratitude doesn't need to be reserved only for momentous occasions, feeling grateful for simple things is just as powerful. And, the practice of reflecting on gratitude each evening helps you identify and multiply the good things in your life.

The journal pages were created to prompt your thinking, but don't overthink. Write whatever comes to mind, without censoring or judging. Don't worry about writing too much or too little, and don't worry about repeating thoughts and ideas. The journal is your tool. Use it in a way that works best for you. Spending just ten minutes in the morning and evening in a contemplative pause can help you be more mindful, focused, and calm. Let the practice of pausing be a source of peace and encouragement, a few minutes just for you.

Share your journey with other educators using #10MPforTs

When something hard happens,
I pause
and take a breath.
When something good happens,
I pause
and take it in.
A pause is powerful.

— Julie

DATE_____   MORNING

How do I want my students to feel today?

How do I want To Feel Today?

What is my intention for the day?

What Do I Want to accomplish today?

Date_____   Evening

What were my students' Wins today?

_____

_____

what were my wins Today?

_____

_____

What AM I learning?

_____

_____

_____

What made me feel grateful today?

_____

_____

_____

_____

_____

DATE_____   MORNING

HOW DO I WANT MY STUDENTS TO FEEL TODAY?

_____
_____

HOW DO I WANT TO FEEL TODAY?

_____
_____

WHAT IS MY INTENTION FOR THE DAY?

_____
_____
_____

WHAT DO I WANT TO ACCOMPLISH TODAY?

_____
_____
_____
_____
_____

Date _____   Evening

What were my students' Wins today?

_____

_____

what were my wins Today?

_____

_____

What AM i learning?

_____

_____

_____

What made me feel grateful today?

_____

_____

_____

_____

_____

Date _____   Morning

How do I want my students to feel today?

_____

_____

How do I want To Feel Today?

_____

_____

What is my intention for the day?

_____

_____

_____

What Do I Want to accomplish today?

_____

_____

_____

_____

_____

Date_____   Evening

What were my students' Wins today?

----

what were my wins Today?

What AM i learning?

What made me feel grateful today?

Date_____   Morning

How do I want my students to feel today?

How do I want To Feel Today?

What is my intention for the day?

What Do I Want to accomplish today?

Date _____   Evening

What were my students' Wins today?

_____

_____

what were my wins Today?

_____

_____

What AM i learning?

_____

_____

_____

What made me feel grateful today?

_____

_____

_____

_____

Date _ _ _ _ _ _ _ _ _   Morning

How do I want my students to feel today?

_ _

_ _

How do I want To Feel Today?

_ _

_ _

What is my intention for the day?

_ _

_ _

_ _

What Do I Want to accomplish today?

_ _

_ _

_ _

_ _

_ _

Date _____   Evening

What were my students' Wins today?

_____

_____

what were my wins Today?

_____

_____

What AM i learning?

_____

_____

_____

What made me feel grateful today?

_____

_____

_____

_____

_____

Date_____   Morning

How do I want my students to feel today?

_____
_____

How do I want To Feel Today?

_____
_____

What is my intention for the day?

_____
_____
_____

What Do I Want to accomplish today?

_____
_____
_____
_____
_____

DATE _____   EVENING

WHAT WERE MY STUDENTS' WINS TODAY?

_____

_____

WHAT WERE MY WINS TODAY?

_____

_____

WHAT AM I LEARNING?

_____

_____

_____

WHAT MADE ME FEEL GRATEFUL TODAY?

_____

_____

_____

_____

_____

Date _____   Morning

How do I want my students to feel today?

_____

_____

How do I want To Feel Today?

_____

_____

What is my intention for the day?

_____

_____

_____

What Do I Want to accomplish today?

_____

_____

_____

_____

_____

Date_____   Evening

What were my students' Wins today?

_____

_____

what were my wins Today?

_____

_____

What AM i learning?

_____

_____

_____

What made me feel grateful today?

_____

_____

_____

_____

_____

Date_____   Morning

How do I want my students to feel today?

How do I want To Feel Today?

What is my intention for the day?

What Do I Want to accomplish today?

Date _ _ _ _ _ _ _ _ _   Evening

What were my students' Wins today?

_ _

_ _

what were my wins Today?

_ _

_ _

What AM i learning?

_ _

_ _

_ _

What made me feel grateful today?

_ _

_ _

_ _

_ _

Date_____   Morning

How do I want my students to feel today?

How do I want To Feel Today?

What is my intention for the day?

What Do I Want to accomplish today?

Date _____   Evening

What were my students' Wins today?

_____

_____

what were my wins Today?

_____

_____

What AM i learning?

_____

_____

_____

What made me feel grateful today?

_____

_____

_____

_____

_____

Date_____   Morning

How do I want my students to feel today?

How do I want To Feel Today?

What is my intention for the day?

What Do I Want to accomplish today?

Date _____   Evening

What were my students' Wins today?

_____

_____

what were my wins Today?

_____

_____

What AM i learning?

_____

_____

_____

What made me feel grateful today?

_____

_____

_____

_____

_____

DATE _____   MORNING

How do I want my students to feel today?

_____

_____

How do I want To Feel Today?

_____

_____

What is my intention for the day?

_____

_____

_____

What Do I Want to accomplish today?

_____

_____

_____

_____

_____

Date _____   Evening

What were my students' Wins today?

_____

_____

what were my wins Today?

_____

_____

What AM i learning?

_____

_____

_____

What made me feel grateful today?

_____

_____

_____

_____

_____

Date_____   Morning

How do I want my students to feel today?

_____

_____

How do I want To Feel Today?

_____

_____

What is my intention for the day?

_____

_____

_____

What Do I Want to accomplish today?

_____

_____

_____

_____

_____

Date _ _ _ _ _ _ _ _ _ _   Evening

What were my students' Wins today?

_ _

_ _

what were my wins Today?

_ _

_ _

What AM i learning?

_ _

_ _

_ _

What made me feel grateful today?

_ _

_ _

_ _

_ _

Date _____   Morning

How do I want my students to feel today?

How do I want To Feel Today?

What is my intention for the day?

What Do I Want to accomplish today?

DATE _____   EVENING

WHAT WERE MY STUDENTS' WINS TODAY?

_____

_____

WHAT WERE MY WINS TODAY?

_____

_____

WHAT AM I LEARNING?

_____

_____

_____

WHAT MADE ME FEEL GRATEFUL TODAY?

_____

_____

_____

_____

_____

Date _____   Morning

How do I want my students to feel today?

How do I want To Feel Today?

What is my intention for the day?

What Do I Want to accomplish today?

DATE _____   EVENING

WHAT WERE MY STUDENTS' WINS TODAY?

_____

_____

WHAT WERE MY WINS TODAY?

_____

_____

WHAT AM I LEARNING?

_____

_____

_____

WHAT MADE ME FEEL GRATEFUL TODAY?

_____

_____

_____

_____

_____

Date _ _ _ _ _ _ _ _ _   Morning

How do I want my students to feel today?

_ _

_ _

How do I want To Feel Today?

_ _

_ _

What is my intention for the day?

_ _

_ _

_ _

What Do I Want to accomplish today?

_ _

_ _

_ _

_ _

_ _

Date_____   Evening

What were my students' Wins today?

_____

_____

what were my wins Today?

_____

_____

What AM i learning?

_____

_____

_____

What made me feel grateful today?

_____

_____

_____

_____

_____

Date_____   MORNING

How do I want my students to feel today?

How do I want To Feel Today?

What is my intention for the day?

What Do I Want to accomplish today?

Date _ _ _ _ _ _ _ _ _ _   Evening

What were my students' Wins today?

_ _

_ _

what were my wins Today?

_ _

_ _

What AM i learning?

_ _

_ _

_ _

What made me feel grateful today?

_ _

_ _

_ _

_ _

_ _

Date _ _ _ _ _ _ _ _ _   Morning

How do I want my students to feel today?

_ _

_ _

How do I want To Feel Today?

_ _

_ _

What is my intention for the day?

_ _

_ _

_ _

What Do I Want to accomplish today?

_ _

_ _

_ _

_ _

_ _

Date_____   Evening

What were my students' Wins today?

----

what were my wins Today?

What AM I learning?

What made me feel grateful today?

Date_____   Morning

How do I want my students to feel today?

_____

_____

How do I want To Feel Today?

_____

_____

What is my intention for the day?

_____

_____

_____

What Do I Want to accomplish today?

_____

_____

_____

_____

_____

Date _____   Evening

What were my students' Wins today?

_____

_____

what were my wins Today?

_____

_____

What AM i learning?

_____

_____

_____

What made me feel grateful today?

_____

_____

_____

_____

_____

DATE_____   MORNING

How do I want my students to feel today?

_____

_____

How do I want To Feel Today?

_____

_____

What is my intention for the day?

_____

_____

_____

What Do I Want to accomplish today?

_____

_____

_____

_____

_____

Date _ _ _ _ _ _ _ _ _ _   EVENING

WHAT WERE MY STUDENTS' WINS TODAY?

_ _

_ _

WHAT WERE MY WINS TODAY?

_ _

_ _

WHAT AM I LEARNING?

_ _

_ _

_ _

WHAT MADE ME FEEL GRATEFUL TODAY?

_ _

_ _

_ _

_ _

_ _

DATE_____   MORNING

HOW DO I WANT MY STUDENTS TO FEEL TODAY?

_____

_____

HOW DO I WANT TO FEEL TODAY?

_____

_____

WHAT IS MY INTENTION FOR THE DAY?

_____

_____

_____

WHAT DO I WANT TO ACCOMPLISH TODAY?

_____

_____

_____

_____

_____

Date_____   Evening

What were my students' Wins today?

_____

_____

what were my wins Today?

_____

_____

What AM i learning?

_____

_____

_____

What made me feel grateful today?

_____

_____

_____

_____

_____

Date _ _ _ _ _ _ _ _ _ _   Morning

How do I want my students to feel today?

_____

_____

How do I want To Feel Today?

_____

_____

What is my intention for the day?

_____

_____

_____

What Do I Want to accomplish today?

_____

_____

_____

_____

_____

Date _ _ _ _ _ _ _ _ _   Evening

What were my students' Wins today?

_ _

_ _

what were my wins Today?

_ _

_ _

What AM i learning?

_ _

_ _

_ _

What made me feel grateful today?

_ _

_ _

_ _

_ _

_ _

Date _____   Morning

How do I want my students to feel today?

How do I want To Feel Today?

What is my intention for the day?

What Do I Want to accomplish today?

Date _ _ _ _ _ _ _ _ _   Evening

What were my students' Wins today?

_____

_____

what were my wins Today?

_____

_____

What AM i learning?

_____

_____

_____

What made me feel grateful today?

_____

_____

_____

_____

_____

DATE _____   MORNING

How do I want my students to feel today?

_____

_____

How do I want To Feel Today?

_____

_____

What is my intention for the day?

_____

_____

_____

What Do I Want to accomplish today?

_____

_____

_____

_____

_____

Date _____   Evening

What were my students' Wins today?

_____

_____

what were my wins Today?

_____

_____

What AM i learning?

_____

_____

_____

What made me feel grateful today?

_____

_____

_____

_____

_____

DATE_____   MORNING

How do I want my students to feel today?

_____
_____

How do I want To Feel Today?

_____
_____

What is my intention for the day?

_____
_____
_____

What Do I Want to accomplish today?

_____
_____
_____
_____
_____

Date _ _ _ _ _ _ _ _ _   Evening

What were my students' Wins today?

_ _

_ _

what were my wins Today?

_ _

_ _

What AM i learning?

_ _

_ _

_ _

What made me feel grateful today?

_ _

_ _

_ _

_ _

DATE_____   MORNING

How do I want my students to feel today?

How do I want To Feel Today?

What is my intention for the day?

What Do I Want to accomplish today?

Date_____   Evening

What were my students' wins today?

_____

_____

what were my wins Today?

_____

_____

What AM i learning?

_____

_____

_____

What made me feel grateful today?

_____

_____

_____

_____

_____

Date_____   Morning

How do I want my students to feel today?

How do I want To Feel Today?

What is my intention for the day?

What Do I Want to accomplish today?

Date _ _ _ _ _ _ _ _ _   Evening

What were my students' Wins today?

_____

_____

what were my wins Today?

_____

_____

What AM i learning?

_____

_____

_____

What made me feel grateful today?

_____

_____

_____

_____

_____

Date _ _ _ _ _ _ _ _ _ _   Morning

How do I want my students to feel today?

_ _

_ _

How do I want To Feel Today?

_ _

_ _

What is my intention for the day?

_ _

_ _

_ _

What Do I Want to accomplish today?

_ _

_ _

_ _

_ _

_ _

Date_____   Evening

What were my students' Wins today?

_____

_____

what were my wins Today?

_____

_____

What AM I learning?

_____

_____

_____

What made me feel grateful today?

_____

_____

_____

_____

_____

Date_____   MORNING

How do I want my students to feel today?

_____

_____

How do I want To Feel Today?

_____

_____

What is my intention for the day?

_____

_____

_____

What Do I Want to accomplish today?

_____

_____

_____

_____

_____

DATE _____   EVENING

WHAT WERE MY STUDENTS' WINS TODAY?

WHAT WERE MY WINS TODAY?

WHAT AM I LEARNING?

WHAT MADE ME FEEL GRATEFUL TODAY?

Date _ _ _ _ _ _ _ _ _ _   MORNING

How do I want my students to feel today?

_ _

_ _

How do I want To Feel Today?

_ _

_ _

What is my intention for the day?

_ _

_ _

_ _

What Do I Want to accomplish today?

_ _

_ _

_ _

_ _

Date _ _ _ _ _ _ _ _ _   Evening

What were my students' Wins today?

_ _

_ _

what were my wins Today?

_ _

_ _

What AM i learning?

_ _

_ _

_ _

What made me feel grateful today?

_ _

_ _

_ _

_ _

_ _

Date_____   Morning

How do I want my students to feel today?

How do I want To Feel Today?

What is my intention for the day?

What Do I Want to accomplish today?

Date _ _ _ _ _ _ _ _ _   Evening

What were my students' Wins today?

_____

_____

what were my wins Today?

_____

_____

What AM i learning?

_____

_____

_____

What made me feel grateful today?

_____

_____

_____

_____

_____

Date_____   Morning

How do I want my students to feel today?

_____

_____

How do I want To Feel Today?

_____

_____

What is my intention for the day?

_____

_____

_____

What Do I Want to accomplish today?

_____

_____

_____

_____

Date _____   Evening

What were my students' Wins today?

_____

_____

what were my wins Today?

_____

_____

What AM i learning?

_____

_____

_____

What made me feel grateful today?

_____

_____

_____

_____

_____

Date_____   Morning

How do I want my students to feel today?

How do I want To Feel Today?

What is my intention for the day?

What Do I Want to accomplish today?

Date _ _ _ _ _ _ _ _ _   Evening

What were my students' Wins today?

_____

_____

what were my wins Today?

_____

_____

What AM i learning?

_____

_____

_____

What made me feel grateful today?

_____

_____

_____

_____

_____

Date _____   Morning

How do I want my students to feel today?

How do I want To Feel Today?

What is my intention for the day?

What Do I Want to accomplish today?

Date_____   Evening

What were my students' Wins today?

----

what were my wins Today?

What AM i learning?

What made me feel grateful today?

Date_____   Morning

How do I want my students to feel today?

_____

_____

How do I want To Feel Today?

_____

_____

What is my intention for the day?

_____

_____

_____

What Do I Want to accomplish today?

_____

_____

_____

_____

_____

Date _____   Evening

What were my students' Wins today?

_____

_____

what were my wins Today?

_____

_____

What AM i learning?

_____

_____

_____

What made me feel grateful today?

_____

_____

_____

_____

_____

Date_____   Morning

How do I want my students to feel today?

How do I want To Feel Today?

What is my intention for the day?

What Do I Want to accomplish today?

Date_____   Evening

What were my students' Wins today?

_____

_____

what were my wins Today?

_____

_____

What AM i learning?

_____

_____

_____

What made me feel grateful today?

_____

_____

_____

_____

Date_____   Morning

How do I want my students to feel today?

How do I want To Feel Today?

What is my intention for the day?

What Do I Want to accomplish today?

DATE _ _ _ _ _ _ _ _ _   EVENING

WHAT WERE MY STUDENTS' WINS TODAY?

WHAT WERE MY WINS TODAY?

WHAT AM I LEARNING?

WHAT MADE ME FEEL GRATEFUL TODAY?

Date _ _ _ _ _ _ _ _ _   Morning

How do I want my students to feel today?

_ _

_ _

How do I want To Feel Today?

_ _

_ _

What is my intention for the day?

_ _

_ _

_ _

What Do I Want to accomplish today?

_ _

_ _

_ _

_ _

_ _

Date _ _ _ _ _ _ _ _ _   Evening

What were my students' Wins today?

_ _

_ _

what were my wins Today?

_ _

_ _

What AM i learning?

_ _

_ _

_ _

What made me feel grateful today?

_ _

_ _

_ _

_ _

Date_____   MORNING

How do I want my students to feel today?

_____

_____

How do I want To Feel Today?

_____

_____

What is my intention for the day?

_____

_____

_____

What Do I Want to accomplish today?

_____

_____

_____

_____

_____

Date _____   Evening

What were my students' Wins today?

_____
_____

what were my wins Today?

_____
_____

What AM i learning?

_____
_____
_____

What made me feel grateful today?

_____
_____
_____
_____

Date_____   Morning

How do I want my students to feel today?

How do I want To Feel Today?

What is my intention for the day?

What Do I Want to accomplish today?

Date_____   Evening

What were my students' Wins today?

_____

_____

what were my wins Today?

_____

_____

What AM I learning?

_____

_____

_____

What made me feel grateful today?

_____

_____

_____

_____

_____

Date_____   Morning

How do I want my students to feel today?

How do I want To Feel Today?

What is my intention for the day?

What Do I Want to accomplish today?

DATE _ _ _ _ _ _ _ _ _ _   EVENING

WHAT WERE MY STUDENTS' WINS TODAY?

_ _

_ _

WHAT WERE MY WINS TODAY?

_ _

_ _

WHAT AM I LEARNING?

_ _

_ _

_ _

WHAT MADE ME FEEL GRATEFUL TODAY?

_ _

_ _

_ _

_ _

_ _

DATE _ _ _ _ _ _ _ _ _   MORNING

How do I want my students to feel today?

_____

_____

How do I want To Feel Today?

_____

_____

What is my intention for the day?

_____

_____

_____

What Do I Want to accomplish today?

_____

_____

_____

_____

_____

Date _ _ _ _ _ _ _ _ _   Evening

What were my students' Wins today?

_____

_____

what were my wins Today?

_____

_____

What AM i learning?

_____

_____

_____

What made me feel grateful today?

_____

_____

_____

_____

_____

DATE_____   MORNING

HOW DO I WANT MY STUDENTS TO FEEL TODAY?

_____

_____

HOW DO I WANT TO FEEL TODAY?

_____

_____

WHAT IS MY INTENTION FOR THE DAY?

_____

_____

_____

WHAT DO I WANT TO ACCOMPLISH TODAY?

_____

_____

_____

_____

_____

Date _____   Evening

What were my students' Wins today?

_____

_____

what were my wins Today?

_____

_____

What AM i learning?

_____

_____

_____

What made me feel grateful today?

_____

_____

_____

_____

_____

DATE _____   MORNING

How do I want my students to feel today?

_____

_____

How do I want To Feel Today?

_____

_____

What is my intention for the day?

_____

_____

_____

What Do I Want to accomplish today?

_____

_____

_____

_____

_____

Date_____   Evening

What were my students' Wins today?

----

what were my wins Today?

What AM i learning?

What made me feel grateful today?

Date_____   MORNING

How do I want my students to feel today?

_____

_____

How do I want To Feel Today?

_____

_____

What is my intention for the day?

___'_____

_____

_____

What Do I Want to accomplish today?

_____

_____

_____

_____

_____

Date _ _ _ _ _ _ _ _ _   Evening

What were my students' Wins today?

_ _

_ _

what were my wins Today?

_ _

_ _

What AM i learning?

_ _

_ _

_ _

What made me feel grateful today?

_ _

_ _

_ _

_ _

Date _____   Morning

How do I want my students to feel today?

_____

_____

How do I want To Feel Today?

_____

_____

What is my intention for the day?

_____

_____

_____

What Do I Want to accomplish today?

_____

_____

_____

_____

_____

Date _ _ _ _ _ _ _ _ _   Evening

What were my students' Wins today?

_____

_____

what were my wins Today?

_____

_____

What AM I learning?

_____

_____

_____

What made me feel grateful today?

_____

_____

_____

_____

DATE_____   MORNING

How do I want my students to feel today?

_____

_____

How do I want To Feel Today?

_____

_____

What is my intention for the day?

_____

_____

_____

What Do I Want to accomplish today?

_____

_____

_____

_____

_____

Date _ _ _ _ _ _ _ _ _ _   Evening

What were my students' Wins today?

_ _

_ _

what were my wins Today?

_ _

_ _

What AM i learning?

_ _

_ _

_ _

What made me feel grateful today?

_ _

_ _

_ _

_ _

Date _____   Morning

How do I want my students to feel today?

_____

_____

How do I want To Feel Today?

_____

_____

What is my intention for the day?

_____

_____

_____

What Do I Want to accomplish today?

_____

_____

_____

_____

_____

Date _____   Evening

What were my students' Wins today?

_____

_____

what were my wins Today?

_____

_____

What AM i learning?

_____

_____

_____

What made me feel grateful today?

_____

_____

_____

_____

_____

Date _____   Morning

How do I want my students to feel today?

_____

_____

How do I want To Feel Today?

_____

_____

What is my intention for the day?

_____

_____

_____

What Do I Want to accomplish today?

_____

_____

_____

_____

_____

Date _____   Evening

What were my students' Wins today?

_____

_____

what were my wins Today?

_____

_____

What AM i learning?

_____

_____

_____

What made me feel grateful today?

_____

_____

_____

_____

_____

DATE_____   MORNING

How do I want my students to feel today?

How do I want To Feel Today?

What is my intention for the day?

What Do I Want to accomplish today?

Date_____   Evening

What were my students' Wins today?

_____

_____

what were my wins Today?

_____

_____

What AM i learning?

_____

_____

_____

What made me feel grateful today?

_____

_____

_____

_____

_____

Date_____   Morning

How do I want my students to feel today?

How do I want To Feel Today?

What is my intention for the day?

What Do I Want to accomplish today?

Date_____   Evening

What were my students' Wins today?

_____

_____

what were my wins Today?

_____

_____

What AM i learning?

_____

_____

_____

What made me feel grateful today?

_____

_____

_____

_____

_____

Date _ _ _ _ _ _ _ _ _ _   Morning

How do I want my students to feel today?

_ _

_ _

How do I want To Feel Today?

_ _

_ _

What is my intention for the day?

_ _

_ _

_ _

What Do I Want to accomplish today?

_ _

_ _

_ _

_ _

_ _

Date _ _ _ _ _ _ _ _ _   Evening

What were my students' Wins today?

_ _

_ _

what were my wins Today?

_ _

_ _

What AM i learning?

_ _

_ _

_ _

What made me feel grateful today?

_ _

_ _

_ _

_ _

_ _

Date_____   Morning

How do I want my students to feel today?

How do I want To Feel Today?

What is my intention for the day?

What Do I Want to accomplish today?

Date _ _ _ _ _ _ _ _ _   Evening

What were my students' Wins today?

_ _

_ _

what were my wins Today?

_ _

_ _

What AM i learning?

_ _

_ _

_ _

What made me feel grateful today?

_ _

_ _

_ _

_ _

_ _

Date_____   Morning

How do I want my students to feel today?

_____

_____

How do I want To Feel Today?

_____

_____

What is my intention for the day?

_____

_____

_____

What Do I Want to accomplish today?

_____

_____

_____

_____

Date _ _ _ _ _ _ _ _ _   Evening

What were my students' Wins today?

_ _

_ _

What were my wins Today?

_ _

_ _

What AM i learning?

_ _

_ _

_ _

What made me feel grateful today?

_ _

_ _

_ _

_ _

_ _

Date _ _ _ _ _ _ _ _ _ _   Morning

How do I want my students to feel today?

_____

_____

How do I want To Feel Today?

_____

_____

What is my intention for the day?

_____

_____

_____

What Do I Want to accomplish today?

_____

_____

_____

_____

Date _____   Evening

What were my students' wins today?

_____

_____

what were my wins today?

_____

_____

What am I learning?

_____

_____

_____

What made me feel grateful today?

_____

_____

_____

_____

_____

Date_____   Morning

How do I want my students to feel today?

_____

_____

How do I want To Feel Today?

_____

_____

What is my intention for the day?

_____

_____

_____

What Do I Want to accomplish today?

_____

_____

_____

_____

_____

Date_____   Evening

What were my students' Wins today?

_____

_____

what were my wins Today?

_____

_____

What AM i learning?

_____

_____

_____

What made me feel grateful today?

_____

_____

_____

_____

Date_____   Morning

How do I want my students to feel today?

How do I want To Feel Today?

What is my intention for the day?

What Do I Want to accomplish today?

Date _ _ _ _ _ _ _ _ _   Evening

What were my students' Wins today?

_ _

_ _

what were my wins Today?

_ _

_ _

What AM i learning?

_ _

_ _

_ _

What made me feel grateful today?

_ _

_ _

_ _

_ _

_ _

Date _ _ _ _ _ _ _ _ _ _   Morning

How do I want my students to feel today?

_ _

_ _

How do I want To Feel Today?

_ _

_ _

What is my intention for the day?

_ _

_ _

_ _

What Do I Want to accomplish today?

_ _

_ _

_ _

_ _

_ _

Date_____   Evening

What were my students' Wins today?

_____

_____

what were my wins Today?

_____

_____

What AM i learning?

_____

_____

_____

What made me feel grateful today?

_____

_____

_____

_____

_____

Date_____   Morning

How do I want my students to feel today?

How do I want To Feel Today?

What is my intention for the day?

What Do I Want to accomplish today?

Date _ _ _ _ _ _ _ _ _   Evening

What were my students' Wins today?

_____

_____

what were my wins Today?

_____

_____

What AM i learning?

_____

_____

_____

What made me feel grateful today?

_____

_____

_____

_____

_____

Date _____   Morning

How do I want my students to feel today?

_____

_____

How do I want To Feel Today?

_____

_____

What is my intention for the day?

_____

_____

_____

What Do I Want to accomplish today?

_____

_____

_____

_____

_____

Date _ _ _ _ _ _ _ _ _   Evening

What were my students' Wins today?

_ _

_ _

what were my wins Today?

_ _

_ _

What AM i learning?

_ _

_ _

_ _

What made me feel grateful today?

_ _

_ _

_ _

_ _

Date_____   Morning

How do I want my students to feel today?

How do I want To Feel Today?

What is my intention for the day?

What Do I Want to accomplish today?

Date _ _ _ _ _ _ _ _ _ _   Evening

What were my students' Wins today?

_ _

_ _

what were my wins Today?

_ _

_ _

What AM i learning?

_ _

_ _

_ _

What made me feel grateful today?

_ _

_ _

_ _

_ _

_ _

Date _ _ _ _ _ _ _ _ _ _   MORNING

How do I want my students to feel today?

_ _

_ _

How do I want To Feel Today?

_ _

_ _

What is my intention for the day?

_ _

_ _

_ _

What Do I Want to accomplish today?

_ _

_ _

_ _

_ _

_ _

Date_____   Evening

What were my students' Wins today?

_____

_____

what were my wins Today?

_____

_____

What AM i learning?

_____

_____

_____

What made me feel grateful today?

_____

_____

_____

_____

Date_____   Morning

How do I want my students to feel today?

How do I want To Feel Today?

What is my intention for the day?

What Do I Want to accomplish today?

Date _ _ _ _ _ _ _ _ _ Evening

What were my students' Wins today?

_ _

_ _

what were my wins Today?

_ _

_ _

What AM i learning?

_ _

_ _

_ _

What made me feel grateful today?

_ _

_ _

_ _

_ _

Date_____   Morning

How do I want my students to feel today?

_____

_____

How do I want To Feel Today?

_____

_____

What is my intention for the day?

_____

_____

_____

What Do I Want to accomplish today?

_____

_____

_____

_____

_____

Date_____   Evening

What were my students' Wins today?

_____

_____

what were my wins Today?

_____

_____

What AM i learning?

_____

_____

_____

What made me feel grateful today?

_____

_____

_____

_____

_____

Date_____   Morning

How do I want my students to feel today?

_____

_____

How do I want To Feel Today?

_____

_____

What is my intention for the day?

_____

_____

_____

What Do I Want to accomplish today?

_____

_____

_____

_____

_____

Date _ _ _ _ _ _ _ _ _   Evening

What were my students' Wins today?

_ _

_ _

what were my wins Today?

_ _

_ _

What AM i learning?

_ _

_ _

_ _

What made me feel grateful today?

_ _

_ _

_ _

_ _

Date_____   Morning

How do I want my students to feel today?

_____

_____

How do I want To Feel Today?

_____

_____

What is my intention for the day?

_____

_____

_____

What Do I Want to accomplish today?

_____

_____

_____

_____

_____

Date _____   Evening

What were my students' Wins today?

_____

_____

what were my wins Today?

_____

_____

What AM i learning?

_____

_____

_____

What made me feel grateful today?

_____

_____

_____

_____

_____

Date_____   Morning

How do I want my students to feel today?

_____

_____

How do I want To Feel Today?

_____

_____

What is my intention for the day?

_____

_____

_____

What Do I Want to accomplish today?

_____

_____

_____

_____

_____

Date _____   Evening

What were my students' Wins today?

_____

_____

what were my wins Today?

_____

_____

What AM i learning?

_____

_____

_____

What made me feel grateful today?

_____

_____

_____

_____

_____

Date _____   Morning

How do I want my students to feel today?

How do I want To Feel Today?

What is my intention for the day?

What Do I Want to accomplish today?

Date_____   Evening

What were my students' Wins today?

_____

_____

what were my wins Today?

_____

_____

What AM i learning?

_____

_____

_____

What made me feel grateful today?

_____

_____

_____

_____

_____

Date_____   Morning

How do I want my students to feel today?

_____

_____

How do I want To Feel Today?

_____

_____

What is my intention for the day?

_____

_____

_____

What Do I Want to accomplish today?

_____

_____

_____

_____

_____

Date _ _ _ _ _ _ _ _ _   Evening

What were my students' Wins today?

_____

_____

what were my wins Today?

_____

_____

What AM i learning?

_____

_____

_____

What made me feel grateful today?

_____

_____

_____

_____

_____

Date _____   Morning

How do I want my students to feel today?

_____

_____

How do I want To Feel Today?

_____

_____

What is my intention for the day?

_____

_____

_____

What Do I Want to accomplish today?

_____

_____

_____

_____

_____

Date _____   Evening

What were my students' Wins today?

_____

_____

what were my wins Today?

_____

_____

What AM i learning?

_____

_____

_____

What made me feel grateful today?

_____

_____

_____

_____

_____

Date _ _ _ _ _ _ _ _ _   Morning

How do I want my students to feel today?

_ _

_ _

How do I want To Feel Today?

_ _

_ _

What is my intention for the day?

_ _

_ _

_ _

What Do I Want to accomplish today?

_ _

_ _

_ _

_ _

Date _ _ _ _ _ _ _ _ _   Evening

What were my students' Wins today?

_____

_____

what were my wins Today?

_____

_____

What AM i learning?

_____

_____

_____

What made me feel grateful today?

_____

_____

_____

_____

_____

Date_____   Morning

How do I want my students to feel today?

_____

_____

How do I want To Feel Today?

_____

_____

What is my intention for the day?

_____

_____

_____

What Do I Want to accomplish today?

_____

_____

_____

_____

Date_____   Evening

What were my students' Wins today?

_____

_____

what were my wins Today?

_____

_____

What AM i learning?

_____

_____

_____

What made me feel grateful today?

_____

_____

_____

_____

_____

Date _____   Morning

How do I want my students to feel today?

_____

_____

How do I want To Feel Today?

_____

_____

What is my intention for the day?

_____

_____

_____

What Do I Want to accomplish today?

_____

_____

_____

_____

_____

DATE_____   EVENING

WHAT WERE MY STUDENTS' WINS TODAY?

_____

_____

WHAT WERE MY WINS TODAY?

_____

_____

WHAT AM I LEARNING?

_____

_____

_____

WHAT MADE ME FEEL GRATEFUL TODAY?

_____

_____

_____

_____

_____

DATE_____   MORNING

HOW DO I WANT MY STUDENTS TO FEEL TODAY?

_____

_____

HOW DO I WANT TO FEEL TODAY?

_____

_____

WHAT IS MY INTENTION FOR THE DAY?

_____

_____

_____

WHAT DO I WANT TO ACCOMPLISH TODAY?

_____

_____

_____

_____

_____

Date_____   Evening

What were my students' Wins today?

----

what were my wins Today?

What AM i learning?

What made me feel grateful today?

DATE_____   MORNING

How do I want my students to feel today?

How do I want To Feel Today?

What is my intention for the day?

What Do I Want to accomplish today?

Date _ _ _ _ _ _ _ _ _   Evening

What were my students' Wins today?

_ _

_ _

what were my wins Today?

_ _

_ _

What AM i learning?

_ _

_ _

_ _

What made me feel grateful today?

_ _

_ _

_ _

_ _

Date _____   Morning

How do I want my students to feel today?

How do I want To Feel Today?

What is my intention for the day?

What Do I Want to accomplish today?

Date _____   Evening

What were my students' Wins today?

_____

_____

what were my wins Today?

_____

_____

What AM I learning?

_____

_____

_____

What made me feel grateful today?

_____

_____

_____

_____

_____

Date_____   Morning

How do I want my students to feel today?

_____

_____

How do I want To Feel Today?

_____

_____

What is my intention for the day?

_____

_____

_____

What Do I Want to accomplish today?

_____

_____

_____

_____

_____

DATE _____   EVENING

WHAT WERE MY STUDENTS' WINS TODAY?

_____

_____

WHAT WERE MY WINS TODAY?

_____

_____

WHAT AM I LEARNING?

_____

_____

_____

WHAT MADE ME FEEL GRATEFUL TODAY?

_____

_____

_____

_____

_____

Date _ _ _ _ _ _ _ _ _ _   Morning

How do I want my students to feel today?

_ _

_ _

How do I want To Feel Today?

_ _

_ _

What is my intention for the day?

_ _

_ _

_ _

What Do I Want to accomplish today?

_ _

_ _

_ _

_ _

_ _

Date _ _ _ _ _ _ _ _ _   Evening

What were my students' Wins today?

_ _

_ _

what were my wins Today?

_ _

_ _

What AM i learning?

_ _

_ _

_ _

What made me feel grateful today?

_ _

_ _

_ _

_ _

Date_____   Morning

How do I want my students to feel today?

_____

_____

How do I want To Feel Today?

_____

_____

What is my intention for the day?

_____

_____

_____

What Do I Want to accomplish today?

_____

_____

_____

_____

Date _____   Evening

What were my students' Wins today?

_____

_____

what were my wins Today?

_____

_____

What AM i learning?

_____

_____

_____

What made me feel grateful today?

_____

_____

_____

_____

DATE _ _ _ _ _ _ _ _ _   MORNING

HOW DO I WANT MY STUDENTS TO FEEL TODAY?

_____

_____

HOW DO I WANT TO FEEL TODAY?

_____

_____

WHAT IS MY INTENTION FOR THE DAY?

_____

_____

_____

WHAT DO I WANT TO ACCOMPLISH TODAY?

_____

_____

_____

_____

Date_____   Evening

What were my students' Wins today?

_____

_____

what were my wins Today?

_____

_____

What AM i learning?

_____

_____

_____

What made me feel grateful today?

_____

_____

_____

_____

Date_____   Morning

How do I want my students to feel today?

_____

_____

How do I want To Feel Today?

_____

_____

What is my intention for the day?

_____

_____

_____

What Do I Want to accomplish today?

_____

_____

_____

_____

_____

Date _ _ _ _ _ _ _ _ _   EVENING

WHAT WERE MY STUDENTS' WINS TODAY?

_ _

_ _

WHAT WERE MY WINS TODAY?

_ _

_ _

WHAT AM I LEARNING?

_ _

_ _

_ _

WHAT MADE ME FEEL GRATEFUL TODAY?

_ _

_ _

_ _

_ _

DATE_____   MORNING

HOW DO I WANT MY STUDENTS TO FEEL TODAY?

HOW DO I WANT TO FEEL TODAY?

WHAT IS MY INTENTION FOR THE DAY?

WHAT DO I WANT TO ACCOMPLISH TODAY?

Date_____   Evening

What were my students' Wins today?

_____

_____

what were my wins Today?

_____

_____

What AM i learning?

_____

_____

_____

What made me feel grateful today?

_____

_____

_____

_____

_____

Date _____   Morning

How do I want my students to feel today?

_____

_____

How do I want To Feel Today?

_____

_____

What is my intention for the day?

_____

_____

_____

What Do I Want to accomplish today?

_____

_____

_____

_____

_____

Date _____   Evening

What were my students' Wins today?

_____

_____

what were my wins Today?

_____

_____

What AM i learning?

_____

_____

_____

What made me feel grateful today?

_____

_____

_____

_____

_____

DATE_____   MORNING

How do I want my students to feel today?

How do I want To Feel Today?

What is my intention for the day?

What Do I Want to accomplish today?

Date_____   Evening

What were my students' Wins today?

_____

_____

what were my wins Today?

_____

_____

What AM i learning?

_____

_____

_____

What made me feel grateful today?

_____

_____

_____

_____

_____

Date_____   Morning

How do I want my students to feel today?

How do I want To Feel Today?

What is my intention for the day?

What Do I Want to accomplish today?

Date _____   Evening

What were my students' Wins today?

_____

_____

what were my wins Today?

_____

_____

What AM i learning?

_____

_____

_____

What made me feel grateful today?

_____

_____

_____

_____

_____

Date _ _ _ _ _ _ _ _ _ _   Morning

How do I want my students to feel today?

_____

_____

How do I want To Feel Today?

_____

_____

What is my intention for the day?

_____

_____

_____

What Do I Want to accomplish today?

_____

_____

_____

_____

_____

Date_____   Evening

What were my students' Wins today?

_____

_____

what were my wins Today?

_____

_____

What AM i learning?

_____

_____

_____

What made me feel grateful today?

_____

_____

_____

_____

_____

Date_____   Morning

How do I want my students to feel today?

How do I want To Feel Today?

What is my intention for the day?

What Do I Want to accomplish today?

Date _____   Evening

What were my students' Wins today?

_____

_____

what were my wins Today?

_____

_____

What AM i learning?

_____

_____

_____

What made me feel grateful today?

_____

_____

_____

_____

_____

DATE_____   MORNING

How do I want my students to feel today?

How do I want To Feel Today?

What is my intention for the day?

What Do I Want to accomplish today?

Date_____   Evening

What were my students' Wins today?

_____

_____

what were my wins Today?

_____

_____

What AM i learning?

_____

_____

_____

What made me feel grateful today?

_____

_____

_____

_____

Date _____   Morning

How do I want my students to feel today?

How do I want To Feel Today?

What is my intention for the day?

What Do I Want to accomplish today?

Date _____   Evening

What were my students' Wins today?

_____

_____

what were my wins Today?

_____

_____

What AM i learning?

_____

_____

_____

What made me feel grateful today?

_____

_____

_____

_____

_____

Date_____   Morning

How do I want my students to feel today?

_____

_____

How do I want To Feel Today?

_____

_____

What is my intention for the day?

_____

_____

_____

What Do I Want to accomplish today?

_____

_____

_____

_____

_____

Date_____   Evening

What were my students' Wins today?

_____

_____

what were my wins Today?

_____

_____

What AM i learning?

_____

_____

_____

What made me feel grateful today?

_____

_____

_____

_____

_____

Date_____   Morning

How do I want my students to feel today?

How do I want To Feel Today?

What is my intention for the day?

What Do I Want to accomplish today?

Date _____   Evening

What were my students' Wins today?

_____

_____

what were my wins Today?

_____

_____

What AM i learning?

_____

_____

_____

What made me feel grateful today?

_____

_____

_____

_____

_____

Date _____   Morning

How do I want my students to feel today?

_____

_____

How do I want To Feel Today?

_____

_____

What is my intention for the day?

_____

_____

_____

What Do I Want to accomplish today?

_____

_____

_____

_____

_____

Date _ _ _ _ _ _ _ _ _ _   Evening

What were my students' Wins today?

_ _

_ _

what were my wins Today?

_ _

_ _

What AM i learning?

_ _

_ _

_ _

What made me feel grateful today?

_ _

_ _

_ _

_ _

_ _

Date_____   Morning

How do I want my students to feel today?

How do I want To Feel Today?

What is my intention for the day?

What Do I Want to accomplish today?

Date _ _ _ _ _ _ _ _ _   Evening

What were my students' Wins today?

_ _

_ _

what were my wins Today?

_ _

_ _

What AM i learning?

_ _

_ _

_ _

What made me feel grateful today?

_ _

_ _

_ _

_ _

_ _

Date _ _ _ _ _ _ _ _ _   Morning

How do I want my students to feel today?

_ _

_ _

How do I want To Feel Today?

_ _

_ _

What is my intention for the day?

_ _

_ _

_ _

What Do I Want to accomplish today?

_ _

_ _

_ _

_ _

Date_____   Evening

What were my students' Wins today?

_____
_____

what were my wins Today?

_____
_____

What AM i learning?

_____
_____
_____

What made me feel grateful today?

_____
_____
_____
_____
_____

Date_____   Morning

How do I want my students to feel today?

_____

_____

How do I want To Feel Today?

_____

_____

What is my intention for the day?

_____

_____

_____

What Do I Want to accomplish today?

_____

_____

_____

_____

_____

Date _____   Evening

What were my students' Wins today?

_____

_____

what were my wins Today?

_____

_____

What AM i learning?

_____

_____

_____

What made me feel grateful today?

_____

_____

_____

_____

_____

DATE _ _ _ _ _ _ _ _ _   MORNING

HOW DO I WANT MY STUDENTS TO FEEL TODAY?

_ _

_ _

HOW DO I WANT TO FEEL TODAY?

_ _

_ _

WHAT IS MY INTENTION FOR THE DAY?

_ _

_ _

_ _

WHAT DO I WANT TO ACCOMPLISH TODAY?

_ _

_ _

_ _

_ _

_ _

Date _____   Evening

What were my students' wins today?

_____

_____

what were my wins today?

_____

_____

What am i learning?

_____

_____

_____

What made me feel grateful today?

_____

_____

_____

_____

_____

Date_____   Morning

How do I want my students to feel today?

How do I want To Feel Today?

What is my intention for the day?

What Do I Want to accomplish today?

Date _ _ _ _ _ _ _ _ _   Evening

What were my students' Wins today?

_ _

_ _

what were my wins Today?

_ _

_ _

What AM i learning?

_ _

_ _

_ _

What made me feel grateful today?

_ _

_ _

_ _

_ _

DATE_____   MORNING

How do I want my students to feel today?

_____

_____

How do I want To Feel Today?

_____

_____

What is my intention for the day?

_____

_____

_____

What Do I Want to accomplish today?

_____

_____

_____

_____

_____

Date_____   Evening

What were my students' Wins today?

_____

_____

what were my wins Today?

_____

_____

What AM I learning?

_____

_____

_____

What made me feel grateful today?

_____

_____

_____

_____

_____

Date_____   Morning

How do I want my students to feel today?

How do I want To Feel Today?

What is my intention for the day?

What Do I Want to accomplish today?

Date _ _ _ _ _ _ _ _ _   Evening

What were my students' Wins today?

_ _

_ _

what were my wins Today?

_ _

_ _

What AM i learning?

_ _

_ _

_ _

What made me feel grateful today?

_ _

_ _

_ _

_ _

_ _

Date_____   Morning

How do I want my students to feel today?

How do I want To Feel Today?

What is my intention for the day?

What Do I Want to accomplish today?

Date_____   Evening

What were my students' Wins today?

_____

_____

what were my wins Today?

_____

_____

What AM i learning?

_____

_____

_____

What made me feel grateful today?

_____

_____

_____

_____

_____

Date_____   Morning

How do I want my students to feel today?

How do I want To Feel Today?

What is my intention for the day?

What Do I Want to accomplish today?

DATE _ _ _ _ _ _ _ _ _   EVENING

WHAT WERE MY STUDENTS' WINS TODAY?

_____

_____

WHAT WERE MY WINS TODAY?

_____

_____

WHAT AM I LEARNING?

_____

_____

_____

WHAT MADE ME FEEL GRATEFUL TODAY?

_____

_____

_____

_____

_____

You did it!

For 90 mornings, you decided how you wanted your day to go. You chose a feeling, determined your intention, and decided on actions that would move you toward your goals. For 90 evenings, you reflected on your day, released what wasn't serving you, and identified moments of gratitude. You paused and gave yourself the gift of time and attention. Now take the time to remember where you were when you started this practice, and celebrate who you've become. You have the power to be the educator (and the human) you want to be. Your students (and the whole world) will be better because you invested in becoming your best self.

You can share your journey with other educators on social media with #10MPforTs. And for even more inspiring resources, visit the Chalk and Chances website (chalkandchances.com). It's full of inspirational stories, videos, and tools. May you continue to find joy and fulfillment in your work and in your life.

Check out the Chalk and Chances website: